Omni-U

Revised 2nd edition

Dr. Leon Moss

2nd edition published 2020:

Golden Child Promotions Publishing Ltd

Portland House,
Belmont Business Park,
Durham,
DH1 1TW

9x9x9@goldenchildpromotionspublishing.com

Copyright © 2020 by Dr. Leon Moss.

All rights reserved. No part of this publication may be reproduced, stored in a retrieval system or transmitted in any form or by any means, electronic, mechanical, photocopying, recording, and/or otherwise without prior written permission of the publishers. This book may not be lent, resold, hired out or otherwise disposed of by way of trade in any form, binding or cover other than that in which it is published, without the prior consent of the publishers.

Acknowledgements

Acknowledgment and thanks to Hayley and aspivey5 for the editing, thanks also to mogumash for assisting with the illustrations and a big thanks to hansbarrow who kindly took care of the book cover and formatting. Your help is truly appreciated.

Contents

Acknowledgements iv

Introduction vii

OMNI-U 1

    What is OMNI-U? 1

Divine Reality 6

The Mind 8

Resistance of the Mind 23

Irritants of Daily Life 29

Real or Unreal 33

Dr. Leon Moss

    The Cornea: 34

    The Iris and the Pupil: 35

    The Retina: 36

    The Muscles: 37

What is Light? 40

How is Light Produced? 42

What is Energy? 45

The Other Side 52

Introduction

The purpose of this book is to raise awareness of the highest aspect of self: pure consciousness. This is the underlying reality of all that is. Human beings have lost what used to be a normal part of their consciousness, leaving an unquenchable mind in its place. The only way to stop this global crisis is to transcend. The time is at hand.

This book contains information from the Holy Tablets and other writings by the Supreme Grand Master Teacher and Spiritual

Dr. Leon Moss

Guide Malachi Z. York. This work is dedicated to making him known. Not enough of us know of the injustice that he endures, like all great leaders who have come to liberate the people from ignorance of self and the oppression.

Here, we strive for a harmonious inner and outer world, by removing the concepts and beliefs that keep us divided.

OMNI-U

What is OMNI-U?

'OMNI' is a prefix meaning ALL; as in Omni-present, Omni-potent, and Omni-science.

'U' is phonetically the same as YOU. Therefore, Omni-U speaks to the quantum aspect of ourselves: the immortal self.

'Quantum' is a Latin word for amount and is defined as the smallest possible discrete unit of any physical property, such as energy or matter. It means that all persons, places, and things, are interconnected by a common substance or essence, the smallest bits that are in and around all of us.

When human beings identify the self as the mind (thoughts), body, and person only, we limit our abilities and overall experience. When seeing beyond this limiting concept, yet still experiencing that which witnesses the mind, body, and person, the realization of unlimited potential is recognized.

The root word of 'potential' is potent which means power. Our true power is in the recognition of our true selves.

The term 'human being' is composed of two words: human is the physical aspect of ourselves and being is the underlying reality. The human mammal has needs, wants, and desires, while being is whole, complete, and without want or need.

Human's experience thoughts that generate feelings of fear, greed, attachment, selfishness, hatred, jealousy, loneliness, and so many more. These emotions form negative energy fields over time that lay dormant in the cells of the body; attacking it, ultimately resulting in anxiety, stress, depression, sickness, and diseases (dis-ease). Being is the true essence of all; natural fragrance is harmony, love, joy, wholeness, and wellbeing.

If you could eliminate suffering from your life would you choose to? Most will say yes, of course, but often they do not have enough awareness. As of yet. The purpose of this writing is to expand your awareness of the true

Dr. Leon Moss

essence of all by guiding you into a direct experience of your forgotten self; Omni-U.

You were made human and given the lesser knowledge which controls you.

Once you are out of love and compassion for yourself, then and only then, can you overstand the truth of yourself and the manifested world we reside in.

You are trapped in a state of cause and effect, the world of light. You were madehuman, given the lesser knowledge which controls you.

When thoughts are thoroughly investigated, the knowledge becomes complete. The knowledge being complete makes your thoughts sincere and your heart is rectified, and the human self-cultivated.

Omni-U

With the self-cultivated, the family is regulated.

Divine Reality

The plane of divine reality is the mental spark; the true essence of a being. A spark of divine consciousness, leading to the development of the human soul; being in the likeness of what you call God, Allah, Yahuwah, and many other names. The oldest of which is El Eloh, also known as Anu, meaning He who is above, The Highest, the most glorified and exalted, the light of life in human beings. A divine spark reflected the spark from the source; the Most High, The Highest, manifesting itself as effect. This Light disturbed the supreme balance of darkness. He created individualism, or a focal point, which manifests as there as opposed to here. This spark is within each individual, making them a supreme being onto beings, known as Anunnaqi, angels, and Aluhumaat, then onto human beings, onto human, onto men, onto mammal, onto beast-like man, onto demon, both male and female. For in spirit there is no gender. We are one!

The Mind

Where exactly is your mind? We are not asking where your brain is. We know the brain is an organ inside your skull. It receives and directs our thoughts, enables memory, speech, movement of the arms and legs, throughout our body by way of the central nervous system. However, the brain is tangible, the mind is not. It is etheric in nature and can be viewed as the etheric counterpart of the brain that is connected to the mental where all thoughts are formed. The magnitude of the mind cannot be measured, for it carries all feelings, ideas, and impressions from this life, as well as intuitive knowledge of what is to come. It is the mind that must be corralled and controlled to achieve true peace and union.

The mind acts to fulfill its desires, and it does not care about consequences. It thinks of a pleasant-looking or pleasant-tasting food, and suddenly you must have some. When warned of the poison it contains, the mind's reaction is to disregard the warning and find some excuse to eat it anyway. However, the highest self, which is pure consciousness, is beyond the mind and it is read from the mental. It is the witness of all that is perceived, the plane of truth, and the plane of divine reality. Pure consciousness neither acts or reacts. For all actions and reactions take place in the mind, which received its information from the mental reservoir, appearing and arriving as thought waves. Thought, the most powerful force in the Omni-verse, initiates all action in the brain. An activity carried out on the physical plane is only a mirror of the inner workings of the mind, which humans assume to be reality. The physical environment in which each person lives is only a projection of their minds.

In truth, when the many mental modifications are resisted, one is no longer affected by the comings and goings of the world and self-shines forth in undisturbed purity. When the thought waves are still, the perceiver rests in their own true nature. This state of pure consciousness is only achieved when the mind is no longer modified by the activities of thought waves. When the waves of a lake are stilled, one can see the bottom clearly. Likewise, when the thought waves of the mind subside, one's essential nature becomes clear.

With the surrender of the ego, the individual becomes an instrument in the hands of El Eloh, The Most High. They take neither credit or blame for their actions; for El Eloh does the action. The devote thinks of nothing but El Eloh, The Most High, whom is in All; and El

Dr. Leon Moss

Eloh, The Most High is his or her constant thought wave, filling every mental space.

Control of the mind and annihilation of the ego are essential to all spiritual disciplines, including emotional ones. Even on an essentially emotional path, the intellect must not be neglected. Disregarding it can cause one to devolve into fanaticism. If, on the other hand, it is transcended, the devotee will experience the highest state of supreme devotional ecstasy. Your motivation should be the simple desire to love and to serve El Eloh, The Highest.

Only with this attitude will the ego disappear. One cannot attain liberation until all desires, including spiritual desires themselves, have been burned away. Pure peace is devoid of desire, ignorance, and emotion. Pure love is untied by lust and it is difficult to develop. It extends beyond the desire to touch and embrace their physical form.

If someone calls you a fool, it is only a verbalization, a vibration in the air; but what a thundering thought wave it creates. One simple, unreal, word wreaks havoc, throwing the physical and emotional bodies into chaos, destroying all happiness and peace. You do not become a fool because you are called one. A human does not grow long ears and a tail because we called them a donkey. Yet, it is not unusual for people to react in anger to such statement, which just gives it validity.

The mind attributes meaning to words by which the delicate degree of difference of the words are perceived by the senses or by the mind, giving them a false reality. Our reactions to meaningless vibrations are the cause of countless human troubles. Overreacting and jumping to conclusions are weaknesses of the mind. The thought waves must be restrained at all times.

We must be particularly wary of praise; for this too is verbal delusion; and the ego, forgetfulness of being, is ever ready to pounce on any opportunity to see itself as better or distinguished from others. Not everyone is going to feel the same way as one who bestows a compliment. Inevitably, the pendulum swings in the other direction, and criticism will be heard sooner or later. But true happiness should not rest on praise or abuse; for in all conditions, your true essence is beyond qualities and beyond change.

Just as water may become steam or ice, it still retains its underlying essence. The weaker a person is, the less restrains he or she has over verbal rhetoric. When the mind is unfocused, the perceiver identifies with its modification. Then thought waves arise and there is an immediate tendency to identify with them, and then the thought waves spawn a host of others.

The mind is a slave to its preoccupation, identifying with the same problem wherever it is. The thought waves give rise to countless others, like ripples, all in search of happiness. But in fact, it is only foolishness. For the very rising of the thoughts themselves actually destroys the peace that the mind craves.

It is said that there are five types of thought waves, when actuality there are seven. Some of these are painful and some are not. The seven kinds of thought waves are: right knowledge, erroneous understanding, verbal delusion, sleep, memory, correct perception, interference, and competent testimony, are proof of right knowledge.

Right knowledge, that is knowledge based on facts, can be proved in three ways; but none of the proofs may contradict oneanother. They are evidence, experience, and common sense.

Examine yourself the next time that you are angry or miserable. Reason it out, and note the modification that has been made to your mind. Gaining freedom from verbal delusion is essential to strengthening your mind.

The mind can neither perceive itself nor perceive another mind. If this were the case, there would be complete confusion of the knowledge and the memory of the different minds. The mind is but an instrument. All knowledge comes from beyond the mind, it comes from the mental. Knowledge of itself comes through self-cognition which occurs when the mind is stilled which explains why it cannot perceive itself. When the mind is stilled, it allows the perception of itself through the right knowledge gained by the awareness-self which is then also known as the mind.

Then the mind has full knowledge. Obviously then, it is not intellectualization but meditation that brings self-knowledge.

The mind, filled with innumerable tendencies and desires, acts for the self; for they act in conjunction. Mind is directly associated with the self so it acts for the self, while it is still full of worldly thoughts. Through

Dr. Leon Moss

discrimination, one can clearly overstand that the soul and the mind are not the same.

The world is full of avarice, hypocrisy, flattery, untruth, double-dealing, selfishness, and those who profess to be friends but are often one's greatest enemy. Beware of self-proclaimed friends who only come for money and other comforts when circumstances are affluent; then they disappear when the tide has turned. These fair-weathered friends give their own brand of advice. They waste precious time in useless chatter and pull you off the spiritual path and down to their own level. Of course, most people do not think this is true. They would like to feel that their relationships are genuine and based on truth, and not based on the fear of being alone and the desire for diversion.

One should cut off connections that are not beneficial, and they should trust only the inner voice that dwells in one's heart. They should associate only with those own aspirations for perfection that are uplifting and encouraging.

Useless talking and excessive debating should also be eliminated. Diarrhea of the tongue wastes so much energy that could be utilized for personal development. Too much talking makes a person restless. Just like a tape recorder, it cannot record and play at the same time. The wise speak only a few words and only when necessary, and because of it, they carry the most force.

To help calm, center and discipline the mind, silence should be observed for about two hours a day in addition to the time spent in meditation. In order to be of themost practical value, silence is best practiced at times when there is the most opportunity to talk. People of an intellectual nature are often prone to unnecessary decisions and controversies. A person who is unable to remain quiet becomes involved in heated debates too easily. Too many of which lead to enmity, hostility, and energy drain. When intellectual reasoning is used for metaphysical inquiry, it can lead to the threshold of intuition.

Past this point, however, it is of no use for transcendental matters. They are beyond the reach of reasoning. One must give up arguing, become silent, and look within.

Fault-finding is also a detrimental habit. The mind of a person who is always poking their nose into the affairs of others is always going to be out of control. No one can be introspective when their mind is engaged in these activities . Diligent application to spiritual practice allows no time for managing the affairs of others. Forget the shortcomings of other people, and work to improve yourself first. Life is precious and far too short. No one knows when it will be taken away, or when it will be their last day.

Every minute should be used for much higher purposes rather than gossiping and judging others.

Self-justification is another behavioral weakness to overcome, along with its associated characteristics like: self-assertion, obstinacy, dissimulation, and lying. These weaknesses are very difficult to eliminate once they become established in the framework of the personality. The ego, forgetfulness of being, never admits to its own faults. One lie covers another; an endless succession of vain attempts at self-justification.

Improvements come quickly only when one learns to readily admit their faults, mistakes, and weaknesses. To have a petty mind is to back-bite and try to pull down other people, which are all results of jealousy and ignorance. This can easily be combated and eradicated by always rejoicing in the welfare of others.

Resistance of the Mind

Negative thoughts seem to assail and attack with double force when the person striving for perfection tries to rid him or herself of them. This is just the natural law of resistance. Eventually, they will perish on their own from the spotlight of consciousness shining on them. Negative thoughts cannot stand before positive thoughts, nor can they remain when being observed from the true self. The very fact that undesirable thoughts create a feeling of uneasiness when they arise, indicates growth and maturity, for at one time these thoughts were welcomed in the mind. However, they cannot be driven out forcefully or suddenly, lest they will turn against you with increased energy. They wither away of their own accord when the person persists in his or her practice with tenacity and diligence.

The mind must be watched particularly when relaxed. Negative thoughts must be countered immediately with positive thoughts; for ill thoughts are destroyed by good thoughts. Just as it is easier to stopan intruder at the gate, so it is easier to check a negative thought as soon as it arises. It can be nipped in the bud by sustained spiritual practice.

Omni-U

Awareness of the Omni-U or the witness-self keeps one alert and on guard for the invasion of misguided thoughts.

Good actions and awareness of the misery that arise from negativity are also tools used to purify the mind. Hatred, like anger, is one of the fiercest foes to all seekers of perfection. Like greed or lust, it is insatiable. Though it may temporarily subside, it can burst out again with redoubled force. It is like a contagious disease, infecting one person after another. Contempt, prejudice, and ridicule are all various modes of hatred.

Infatuation and attachments are also serious obstacles because they are subtle but powerful.

When millions of people are killed during a war, a mortal does not weep; yet he or she weeps when his or her spouse dies. This is because infatuation creates the idea of "mine" and the greater the attachment, the greater the pain. When a person speaks of "my wife, my son, or my home," they reveals an attitude of separation from the rest of humanity. So long as there is identification with the ephemeral physical world, little progress can be made on the path of perfection.

Greed, which is closely linked with infatuation, is insatiable and agitates the mind. Even though a person may be a millionaire, he or she schemes to become a billionaire. Greed assumes various subtle forms. Striving for name and fame is also greed

Infatuation, attachments, and greed, are destroyed by vigorous self-inquiry, prolonged meditation, and constant spiritual practice.

Another impediment to perfection is memory or the recalling of past events. To overstand this, assume for a moment that one is meditating in a solitary country setting. If memories of a past holiday arise and the mind is allowed to dwell on them, even for a moment, one will actually experience that event in a past time. This applies to daydreams as well. Looking back to past experiences gives life to the memory picture, reinforces it, and pulls the mind away from its true nature. A supreme being never looks back. This does not mean we should not reflect on the goods of the past. It means to remain in the present moment to realign with reality.

However, listening to the music of your childhood and remembering your mom or dad, grandma or grandad singing or listening to the oldies of their time, the sound waves will

Dr. Leon Moss

reactivate dead brain cells. It's one of the keys to rejuvenation or the fountain of youth. It will make us younger in heart, body, and mind.

However, the total opposite is observed for those elders who listen to new music and are not grounded in the witness self. It will remind you of your age and your speed to death.

Irritants of Daily Life

Unfavorable environments, unfriendly atmospheres, and other obstacles do not necessarily lead to the defeat of our strives towards perfection. Rather, they serve as trials and aids in the development of such strong powers as discrimination, empathy, will, and endurance.

On the other hand, undesirable company is highly disastrous. Such contact fills the mind with useless ideas, hate, racism, sectism, etc. To avoid being pulled into negativity, the seeker of perfection should protect themselves carefully from any distracting influences. People who lie, steal, are greedy, or indulge in back-biting as well as those who pass the time with idle gossiping, should be avoided at all costs. As the elders use to say, 'The more you notice a monkey, the more it will clown.' Avoidance is best.

The term 'undesirable company' includes more than just people. It can be anything that gives rise to negative thoughts, like bad music, dangerous sports, rowdy surroundings, dark parties, gangs, war, murder, books that promote negativity, movies with lots of violence, songs that create discontent, and television programs that center on violence, sensuality, and all other negative vibrations. These things just lead the mind astray and fill it with desires it would not normally have. One should even consider curtailing your reading of some newspapers; for their intent, as well as effect, is to tantalize the mind with waves of unrest and sensationalism. All these distractions draw the mind outward; rather than focus it inwards. They foster the illusion that this world is a solid reality and obscure the supreme truth which underlies all names and forms; the real you, the witness self!

Watch your mind very carefully. Be alert. Do not allow the waves of irritability, jealousy, hatred, and lust disturb you. These evil waves are enemies of peaceful living, meditation, and wisdom. The obstacles on the path of perfection can easily be overcome once an intelligent and comprehensive overstanding of them has been reached. One should always

Dr. Leon Moss

bear in mind that failures are but stumbling stones to success. One must train the mind properly and not be discouraged; for the journey to perfection was never completed through one shadow hour, which you call night.

Real or Unreal

You look at everything around you with your eyes, but are they really what enable you to see?? Well, let us examine the eye and how it functions. This organ is a ball about one inch in diameter, covered by internal fluids. Its movements are controlled by six externally attached muscles. The eye transmits or carries the images that you see to the retina, which then transmits those images to the brain.

Like the rest of the human body, the eye is divided into various parts. The main parts of the eye are as follows:

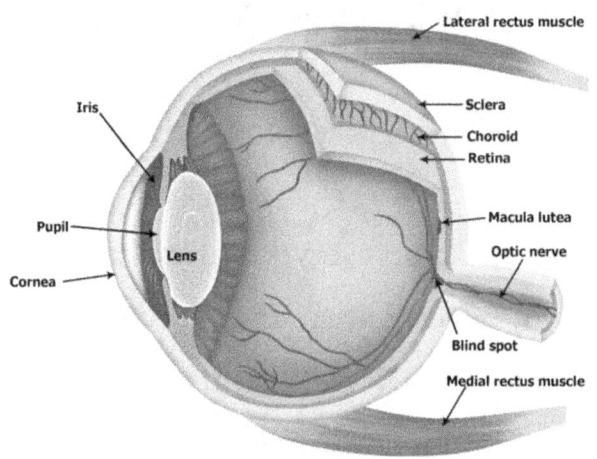

The Cornea:

The cornea is the transparent front of the eye that covers the iris and the pupil. It can be seen by simply looking into a human being's eye. It is the bulge over the pupil.

The Iris and the Pupil:

If you look closely into the eye of a human being, you will see a black dot surrounded by a circle of fine lines. The lines seemingly emerge from the pupil following the pattern of the rays of the sun. The black dot is the pupil and that which surrounds it is called the iris. The iris covers the lens and gives the eye its color, be it black, brown, blue, or green. The amount of light that enters the eye is determined by the iris. It adjusts the diameter of the pupil, (similar to the working of a camera lens) to increase or decrease the amount of light allowed to penetrate the eye. For instance, if you take a light and shine it into the eyes, you will see that the iris will expand in size causing the pupil to shrink. If you remove the light from the eyes, you will see that the iris will decrease making the pupil appear larger.

Dr. Leon Moss

The Retina:

The retina is located inside the back part of the eye. It is, in a sense, the brain's means of exposure to the outer world. The retina is a network of nerves which are an expansion of the optic nerve. These cables, if you will, lead to the brain and can only be seen by way of an ophthalmoscope. When the light of an ophthalmoscope is directed into the eye, it enables a deeper examination of the eye. Planted in the furthest most part of the eye is a yellow disk. This is called the optic disk and is where the optic nerve leaves the eye and enters the brain. The point where the optic nerve enters the eye is called the blind spot. Thus, named because it has no sense receptors to transmit information back to the brain. Before the optic nerve reaches the brain, it divides at the optic chiasma. This is the crossover point where the images from the right eye travel to the left side of the brain, and the images from the left eye travel to the right side of the brain.

The Muscles:

Six muscles are responsible for the movement of the eye. These muscles allow the eye to look forward, as well as move upward and downward, and crosswise. The function of these muscles is what allows us to see what is in front of us as well as in our peripheral vision.

Now I ask you, is it the eye that allows you to see?

When you say, "I see," do you really mean that you are looking at something, or are you saying in actuality that you understand something? Well, let us find out by looking deeper into it. We know that there are various disorders of the eye that creep up unexpectedly and can cause many problems. For instance, when a viral and contagious disease called trachoma causes tissue growth over the cornea, there is a possibility of blindness. However, corneal transplants are performed which can restore vision.

Another disorder of the eye is clouding of the lens. This is called cataracts. Left untreated, this disorder can become severe and result in blindness. Yet, with proper treatment, cataracts can also be defeated.

If the retina becomes detached for one reason or another, you can lose your ability to see. Unless, of course, the retina is sewn back in place at which time you can regain your sight.

But if severe damage is brought upon the optic nerve or visual region of the eye in the brain, the resulting blindness is permanent. Thus, I ask you, is it the organ called the eye that allows you to see, or does the ability to see come from within?

And what about light? Everyone knows that when you step into a dark room you cannot see for a moment or two, but when you switch the light on, you can see. Therefore, is it light that aids you to see?

Let us examine light.

What is Light?

To most, this question is as much as a mystery now as it was in the past. Light is energy. It is specifically called radiant energy because it radiates and shoots forth in a wave motion. It is said that the distance that light travels per second is approximately the same as the time it takes one to walk around the Earth's equator seven times. Light encompasses the seen and the unseen. What we mean by this, is that there is light that you can see, such as daylight, and there is light that you cannot see with the naked eye, such as ultraviolet light (also known as black light), and infrared lights. Even though these can be captured by artificial means.

How is Light Produced?

Light is produced by atoms; so light was created as atoms formed out of supreme darkness: bliss. When these atoms are excited, the pace at which they move increases and thus light is produced. The cause of this excitement may be naturally or artificially induced. The more excited the atoms become, the more energy they give and therefore, more light. The less excited the atoms become, the less energy they give, and therefore the less light, or maybe no light is produced at all. So, light is excitement and chaos; and darkness is peace and tranquility. It is interesting to note that contrary to what you may think, when you see red light the atoms are less excited than blue light's atoms are more excited. Although a red flame is hot, a blue flame is hotter still.

Hence, when this excited wave or energy of light falls on an object, the object reflects, bends, absorbs, or does a combination of all three, which gives the object its appearance and color.

The light is reflected from the object enters the cornea so, it needs persons, places, or things to reflect the light; but darkness exists and has always existed. There, it is refracted (bent) as it goes through the lens of the eye. The refraction causes rays of light to cross within the eye causing , the image of the object to be inverted and projected off the retina. That projected light or radiant energy is then turned into chemical energy by the retina. This means when light reaches the retina, heat, light or both, will be discharged or absorbed by that area of the retina.

What is Energy?

Dr. Leon Moss

There is a great deal of energy flowing throughout the Omni-verse. The energy is seen in the form of light. Light is the visible part of energy. The electromagnetic spectrum is a range of things related by certain characteristics. In this case, the spectrum is made up of energy that travels through space much like a wave that ripples in a pond. Scientifically, the height of the wave is called the amplitude or the height of its intensity. The distance between the peak of one wave and the peak of the next is called the wavelength, and the time per second that it takes a wave to pass through a specific point is the frequency. That spectrum is called electromagnetic because it has an electric and a magnetic field. The electric wave of the electric field is identical in amplitude, wavelength, and frequency as the magnetic waves of the magnetic field, and is thus electromagnetic. The electromagnetic spectrum contains long and short waves.

This brings us into the awareness of the aura or light body of human beings. As we said previously, when an object absorbs light, it will excite its molecules and raise the energy level. When the energy level rises, heat is created. This is why wearing black in the summer makes you very hot, and if you walk barefoot on the pavement, your feet feel like they are on fire. When the light that is absorbed increases, the atoms themselves release energy or light. This process is called phosphorescence. When the atoms of a source absorb energy from the light it, in turn, gives off light. When everyone that walks on this earth was born, they took a breath of life. That breath of life was a breath of light; not the light of a bulb but a light of life-giving, pouring forth, forever emanating, and forever penetrating. This light is what makes us a living soul. It all existed in the darkness before it became things. Light is one of the things in darkness.

As you, the mind, body, person, breathe in and out, this light or spark moves constantly ever interchanging and communicating with the force of the Kosmos/ Omniverse. Not only does it get charged by every breath that you take in, but also by your physical senses (seeing, hearing, smelling, tasting, and feeling), as well as your spiritual senses (crown seat of light, solar plexus, and third eye). Every individual has a rhythm by which their physical body is in tune with the Omniverse. If this rhythm slows down, there is an imbalance and the result is eventually physical weakness. The spark of life keeps the rhythm in tune. Too much spark at one time, however, will speed the rhythm up too quickly and cause a short circuit in the body; but a gradual increase in the strength of the spark and in its intensity, will allow the spark (light, life) to saturate the body until every cell has absorbed it. This process will continue until each cell gives off its own light. A light that diffuses with the soul and the heart. It expands and is expressed in an electromagnetic wave of light that surrounds the entire body. This electromagnetic wave field, beloved Kosmosan, is what is called the aura. This mist is the prototype of the halo or nimbus constantly depicted around the heads of those considered holy, except that it covers the entire being and not merely the head.

Whether asleep or awake, hot or cold, happy or sad, every being is surrounded by this magnetic force field. It contains the ether particles of green light which are waiting to be

Dr. Leon Moss

drawn into the body by the seats. Man's aura contains his spirit, soul, and physical form. The human aura appears up to two or three feet away from the body. The aura may be looked upon as the atmosphere of the body because it reflects the 'real body'; its mental mood, health, and character. It is always present. Its moods are reflected in colors which appear cloud-like or bright and clear according to the mood it is reflecting. Often, one color may totally dominate or cloud out most of the other moods reflected. The purer the person, the more illuminated his or her aura will be. An aura rarely ever stays the same. It reflects the most intricate moods of the person, and they are constantly changing with every thought. Between females and males, the aura is apt to change more in females because women are affected by the planets, their position, and the moon; while men, on the other hand, are not affected by those conditions.

Overall, human beings can control their own thoughts and emotions; thus, controlling the energy sent out, which in turn, controls the energy returned.

The Other Side

Existence in the physical body is but a flash in the life of the soul. The brevity of earthly life becomes more apparent the older a person gets. As the seeker progresses on the path of righteousness, they begin to realize that all of existence is a spiritual experience. The only purpose of moving in and out of physical bodies is to advance toward perfection. Death is simply another spiritual experience of the phase through which the soul passes.

It is also a sickness that can and will be cured. During that period of transition referred to as "death", the body ceases to perform life functions; it's sick.

The physical body is of the gross earth plane. For it comes from and is composed of the elements of the earth. So, the cure is also here. True age should be 120 earth years of earth time for this body (Genesis 6:3). Bad food, air, water, and bad thinking are why it ends before 120 years.

Having served its purpose, the body returns to the earth; but when and how one dies is the key. Even God or Yahuwa or Anu has a time. For it says each day to the Lord Yahweh is like 1,000 years. (Psalms 90:4) (Koran 32:5). Therefore, he has a life span as a beginning and an end.

Dr. Leon Moss

The soul separates to exist on other planes. Earthly existence is but a fraction of the experience. Every person has three bodies: the physical body, the astral body, and the causal body; his or her own trinity. The physical body is also called the food sheath for it is composed of what is eaten. At the end of life, it returns to the food cycle.

The astral body is composed of the vital sheath, which contains all the energy; the mental sheath, which contains all emotions and desires; and the intellectual sheath, which performs the functions of analyzing the thinking.

The casual body is made up of the bliss sheath, for its nature is pure bliss.

The astral body, which interpenetrates and extends 6-8 inches beyond the physical body where it is frequently called the "haalah" or aura. The physical body is the vehicle of the astral and causal bodies; while the soul is to incarnate on earth in order to learn the lesser.

When death comes, the astral body with the ether, the mind, memories, past impressions or thought waves and the senses, which all exist in the astral body, separate from the physical body. They move out of the earth's plane to higher planes; not merely a higher place, but also to higher levels of vibrations where another type of knowledge is gained. When death occurs, the soul, accompanied by the astral body, departs from the physical body to live out its 1000-year life. It travels to different planes according to its fate. The results of good fate may be the enjoyment of heavenly surroundings, while negative fate earns unpleasant experiences beyond the physical plane.

After leaving physical life, the soul's experiences correspond to the afterlife he or she comes to expect. The soul travels to a plane that is most influenced by the last thought.

There can be no doubt that heaven and hell exist; both here and elsewhere, although these are as a state of mind as a solid reality. A person who has been selfish, greedy, or brutal will exist on a lower plane where they must face the memory and effect of those deeds. One who has lived a virtuous life travels to a higher plane to other planets where the soul will have but to think of that which it wants and its desire will automatically manifest from their thoughts. But those who have transcended the idea of heaven rewards and who overstands the nature of birth and rebirth as well as no longer wish to partake of the endless round of material pleasures and pains, travel to even higher planes on to other worlds where everything is of purer and lighter vibrations. There is still pleasure; for these souls will have accumulated much agreeable fate.

Overall the experience is a learning one. This is the working of the mind.

If you feel to leave me a review online, it would be greatly appreciated :9)

Thank you

www.ingramcontent.com/pod-product-compliance
Lightning Source LLC
Chambersburg PA
CBHW071543080526
44588CB00011B/1768